Guess What

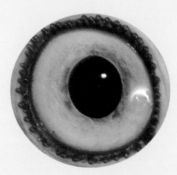

Published in the United States of America by
Cherry Lake Publishing
Ann Arbor, Michigan
www.cherrylakepublishing.com

Content Adviser: Susan Heinrichs Gray
Reading Adviser: Marla Conn, ReadAbility, Inc.
Book Design: Felicia Macheske

Photo Credits: © Eric Isselée/Shutterstock.com, cover, 3, 21, back cover; © Tracy Starr/Shutterstock.com, 1, 4, 8, 11, 18;
© Super Prin/Shutterstock.com, 7; © Nicky Rhodes/Shutterstock.com, 12; © Volodymyr Krasyuk/Shutterstock.com, 15;
© duangnapa_b/Shutterstock.com, 16; © Andrey_Kuzmin/Shutterstock.com, back cover

Library of Congress Cataloging-in-Publication Data

Calhoun, Kelly, author.
 Flashy feathers / Kelly Calhoun.
 pages cm. — (Guess what)
 Summary: "Young children are natural problem solvers and always looking for answers, especially when it involves
animals. Guess What: Flashy Feathers: Macaw provides young curious readers with striking visual clues and simply
written hints. Using the photos and text, readers rely on visual literacy skills, reading, and reasoning as they solve the
animal mystery. Clearly written facts give readers a deeper understanding of how the animal lives. Additional text
features, including a glossary and an index, help students locate information and learn new words."
— Provided by publisher.
 Audience: Ages 5-8.
 Audience: K to grade 3.
 ISBN 978-1-63362-626-3 (hardcover) — ISBN 978-1-63362-716-1 (pbk.) — ISBN 978-1-63362-806-9 (pdf)
— ISBN 978-1-63362-896-0 (ebook)
 1. Macaws—Juvenile literature. [1. Parrots.] I. Title.

QL696.P7C3165 2016
598.7'1—dc23

2015003094

Cherry Lake Publishing would like to acknowledge the work of The Partnership for 21st Century Skills.
Please visit *www.p21.org* for more information.

Printed in the United States of America
Corporate Graphics Inc.

Table of Contents

I can see more **colors** than you.

My body is covered with colorful feathers.

Yak Yak
Yak

I can
imitate
you.

I use my feet to grab things.

I am
smart and
I like
to play!

I have
wings
and can fly.

I have
long tail
feathers.

I use my strong beak for eating.

Do you know what I am?

I'm a Macaw!

About Macaws

1. Macaws can imitate human **voices**.

2. Macaws have strong beaks that are good for crushing nuts and berries.

3. Macaws have bright feathers to help them blend in with fruits and flowers in trees.

4. There are 17 different kinds of macaws.

5. Macaws live in large groups, called flocks.

Glossary

grab (grab) to take hold of something suddeny

imitate (IM-i-tate) to copy or mimic someone or something

smart (smahrt) clever and quick-witted, bright

voices (VOIS-ez) the sounds produced by air passing through the throat and out of the mouth

Index